ALL THE THINGS YOU ARE

Transcriptions and In-Depth Analysis
of Solos by 15 Jazz Greats Playing
Jerome Kern's Classic Song

ALL THE THINGS YOU ARE

Transcriptions and In-Depth Analysis
of Solos by 15 Jazz Greats Playing
Jerome Kern's Classic Song

Joe Albany

Shelly Berg

Dave Brubeck

Tommy Flanagan

Hampton Hawes

Ahmad Jamal

Adam Makowicz

Marian McPartland

Phineas Newborn Jr.

Oscar Peterson

André Previn

Hal Schaeffer

Ralph Sharon

Derek Smith

Cedar Walton

By Gene Rizzo

HAL•LEONARD®
CORPORATION
7777 W. BLUEMOUND RD. P.O. BOX 13819 MILWAUKEE, WI 53213

One more once for Jeanne

ISBN: 978-1-4234-3041-4

Published by:
Hal Leonard Corporation
7777 W. Bluemound Road
P.O. Box 13819
Milwaukee, WI 53213

Printed in the U.S.A.

First Edition

Visit Hal Leonard Online at
www.halleonard.com

CONTENTS

INTRODUCTION

*B*orn in New York City, Jerome Kern (1885–1945) was the first homegrown composer to make a vital contribution to the musical theater. Broadway's romance with the operetta-like confections of Sigmund Romberg, Rudolph Friml, and Victor Herbert—European composers all—ended with the emergence of Kern's distinctly American voice in such stage productions as *Sally* (1920), *Sunny* (1925), *Show Boat* (1928), and *Roberta* (1933). Kern was better trained than most of his Tin Pan Alley contemporaries, and often fretted that his creations might be too complicated to have popular appeal. Yet, despite their sophisticated construction, his songs are among the most enduring, singer-friendly entries in the Great American Songbook.

"All the Things You Are," for example, with its second pass of the A section in another key, its seamless recapitulation of A after a masterful enharmonic change concludes the bridge, and its final soaring bars spun with completely new thematic material, has become one of Kern's best-loved songs, even though it ignores the formal conventions of its time. It first appeared in the score of *Very Warm for May* (1939). The show, a rare Kern flop, closed after 59 performances at reduced ticket prices, but the song rose to the top of the hit parade on New York radio, and was quickly taken up by popular vocalists and dance bands.

The history of "All the Things You Are" as an appealing vehicle for improvisation begins in 1947 with Charlie Parker's recorded interpretation. Devoid of a melody statement, strictly an exploration of its chord changes, Parker felt justified to rename it "Bird of Paradise." Having heard the falconer, the falcons responded, and the song with and/or without its melody became a staple of the jazz repertory. If jazz singers were put off by Oscar Hammerstein's somewhat overstated lyrics, hordes of pianists were drawn to the harmonic challenges of the song.

This book is a study of the boundless riches of "All the Things You Are" as seen through the prisms of 15 outstanding jazz pianists.

AN ANALYSIS OF THE ORIGINAL SHEET MUSIC

*K*ern wisely insisted on absolute fidelity to his harmonizations in the publication of his songs. Most editors would have grounded Kern's adventurous harmonic flights by applying academic constraints whose only justification is the tradition of common practice.

The verse of "All the Things You Are" vindicates Kern's uncompromising position as well as anything in his catalog. It is cast in G major, an unlikely preparation for the refrain's key of F minor. Kern offers two variations of a catchy two-bar phrase before arriving at the dominant chord in the first half of bar 7. Dominant-seventh chords with ear-tweaking alterations complete the section. The catchy phrase returns at bar 9 with a new bass line (beginning on A, the ninth of the chord, no less) moving along to support a variation that seems destined for E minor. Bars 13 through 15 shatter any possibility of this, and end on a resounding full cadence in G major. Oscar Hammerstein has discreetly provided no lyrics for the three quarter note pick-ups that enter the refrain without incident on the wings of a C7 chord.

Kern refuses to be hamstrung by the F minor tonality established in the opening bars of the refrain; his restless theme passes through A♭, D♭, and finally C major within eight bars. C minor, a cat's whisker away, is chosen for the theme's restatement. The unusual procedure of repeating the main strain in a contrasting key appears in other Kern songs—"Pick Yourself Up" (1936) and "Long Ago and Far Away" (1944)—but was never applied so convincingly as in "All the Things You Are."

The epic sweep of a Jerome Kern bridge can be nearly autonomous; the significance of the main strain is seriously challenged (e.g., "Smoke Gets in Your Eyes," "I Won't Dance," "The Way You Look Tonight," "The Song Is You"). In the bridge of "All the Things You Are," Kern is disinclined to compete with his preceding theme and tenderly weaves a pair of imitative phrases through G and E major. (Inexplicably, jazz players ignore the drama of the F♯m7♭5 in bar 5, preferring an unaltered fifth in their voicing of the chord.) Bars 7 and 8 bring about the much-celebrated enharmonic change from an E major to a C augmented chord. A similar enharmonic link between the bridge and the recap can be found in "The Song Is You" (1932), but does not hide its scaffolding as well.

Four bars into the recap a new theme is taken up. An inspired departure from any previous material, it is laced with carefully chosen primary chord tones, yet sounds as spontaneous as bird song. A suspended chord (B♭m7/E♭ in bar 9) anticipates the V-I cadence in A♭ major, the reigning key of the section. The melody's optional ending in the higher octave, harkening back to operetta traditions in the grand manner that no longer prevail on Broadway, is seldom used.

The song is considered the crowning achievement of the composer's last period. In 1945, six years after he wrote it, Kern died of a heart attack on a New York street a few blocks from his suite at the St. Regis Hotel.

ALL THE THINGS YOU ARE

from VERY WARM FOR MAY

Lyrics by OSCAR HAMMERSTEIN II
Music by JEROME KERN

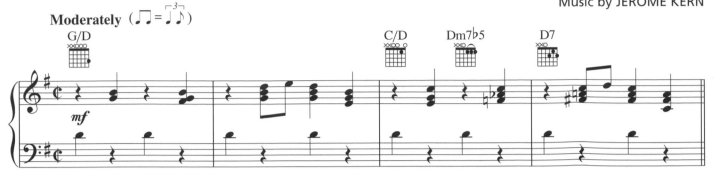

Time and a - gain I've longed for ad - ven - ture, some - thing to make my

heart beat the fast - er. What did I long for? I nev - er real - ly

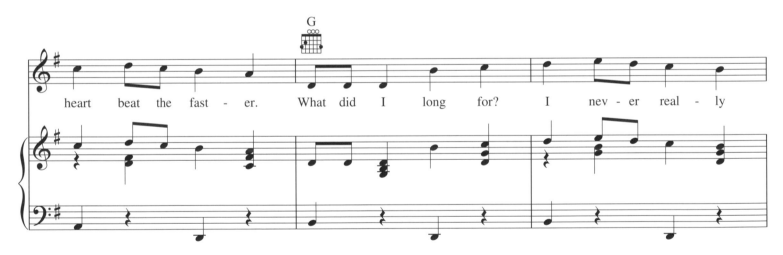

knew.   Find - ing your love, I've found my ad - ven - ture;

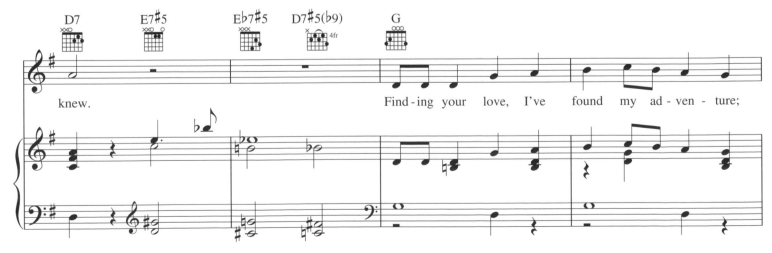

touch - ing your hand, my heart beats the fast - er. All that I want in

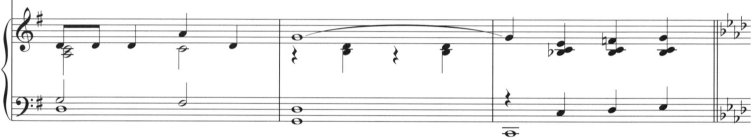

all of this world is you. _____

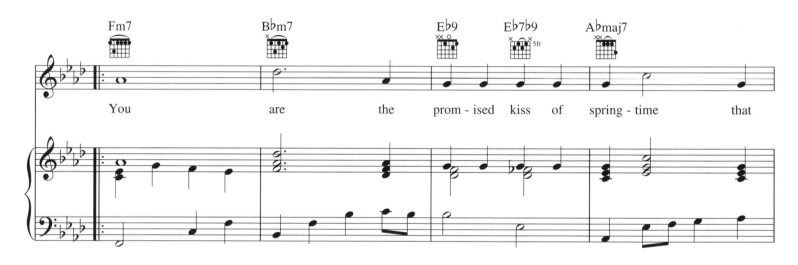

You are the prom - ised kiss of spring - time that

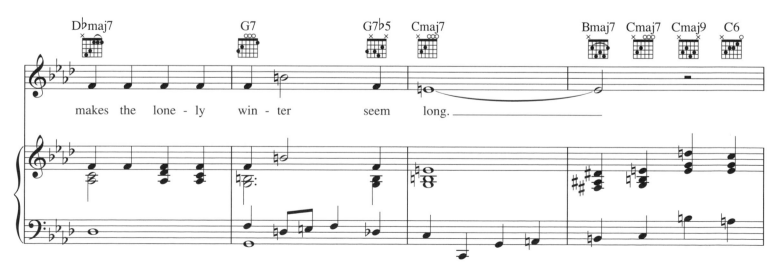

makes the lone - ly win - ter seem long. _____

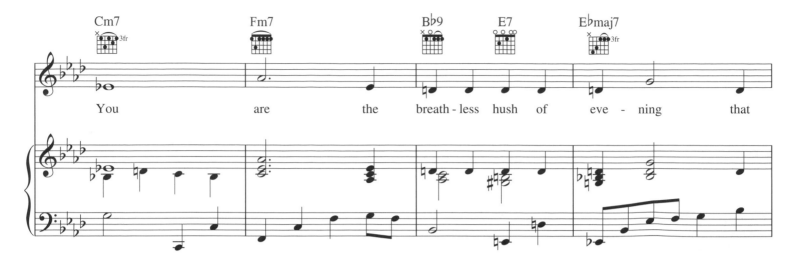

You are the breath-less hush of eve-ning that

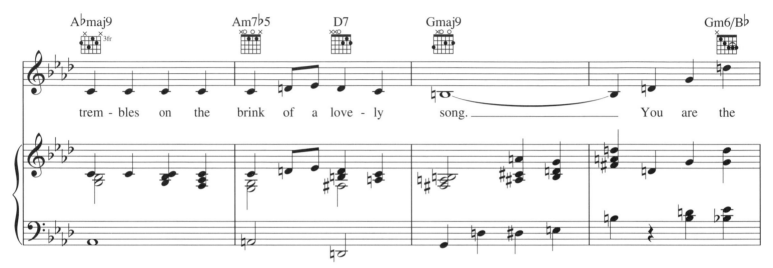

trem-bles on the brink of a love-ly song._____ You are the

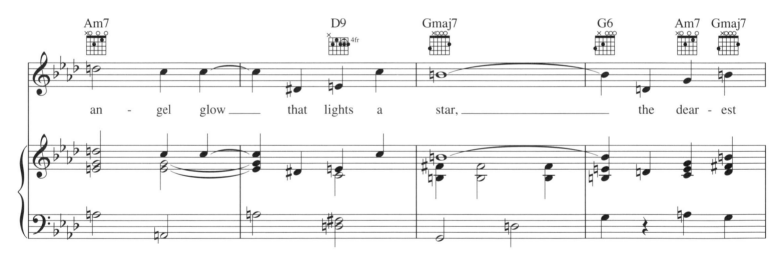

an-gel glow _____ that lights a star, _____ the dear-est

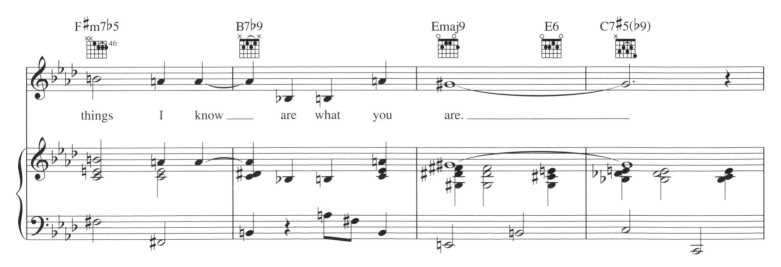

things I know _____ are what you are. _____

Some - day my hap - py arms will hold you, and

some - day I'll know that mo - ment di - vine when

all the things you are, are mine!

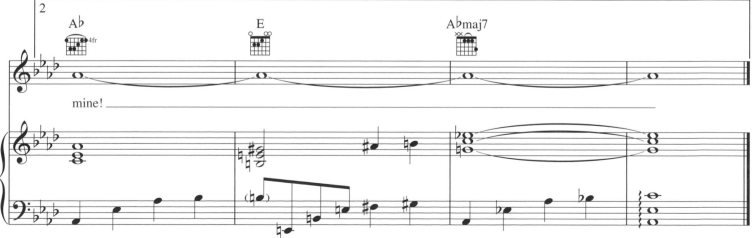

mine!

COMPLETE SOLO TRANSCRIPTIONS
AS PLAYED BY HAMPTON HAWES
AND RALPH SHARON

HAMPTON HAWES'S SOLO

*H*awes's first recordings for the Contemporary label (1955) were bound to include "All the Things You Are." Contemporary's founder, Lester Koenig, had heard Hawes, then little known, play it—no, ignite it—at the Lighthouse in Hermosa Beach, California. Koenig's determination to replicate the performance in his studio did not bear fruit until nearly two years later, but was well worth the wait.

The cutting-edge bebop of the solo's two improvised choruses are preceded by a free rubato statement of the head by the pianist alone (with a nod to Art Tatum), and another presentation joined by the rhythm section at a brisk tempo. Kern's melody is never obscured in spite of added passing tones and rhythmic variations. Hawes, himself an engaging melodist, always managed to pull off this hat trick on theme statements. At letter B, for example, bars 3–6 and 9–15 parapharase the original lines without disfiguring them beyond recognition.

Hawes parts company with the sheet music harmony in the same places throughout the solo, substituting the E♭7 in the third bar of the main strain with an Em7 to A7 progression and exchanging the B diminished chord five bars before the end of each chorus for an F7. The pianist is content to follow Kern's harmonic template except for extensions and some tastefully altered dominants.

It was Hawes's gutsy swinging and creative imagination in performances such as this that put the California native on the top tier of West Coast pianists in the 1950s and beyond. His death in 1977, after many years of substance abuse, is still mourned in the jazz community.

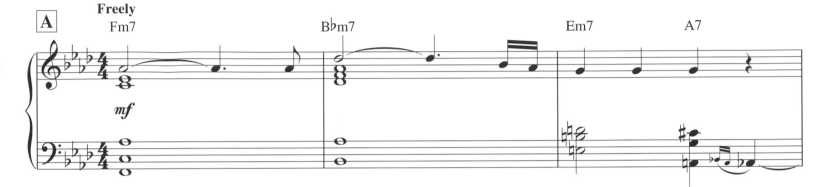

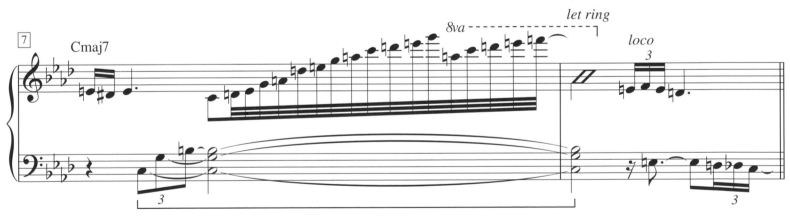

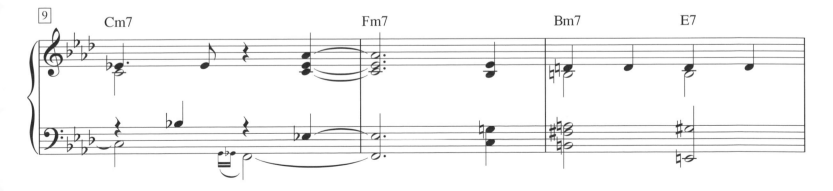

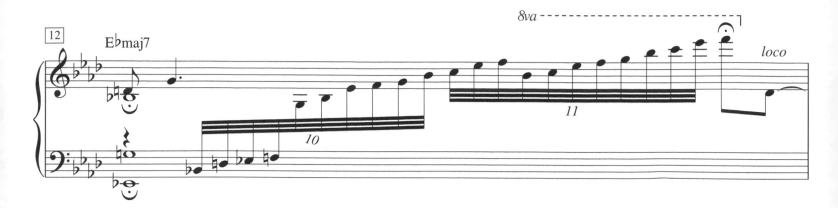

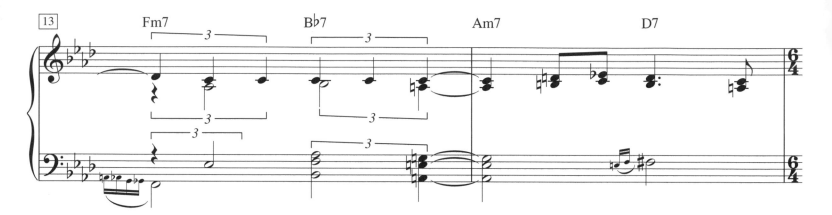

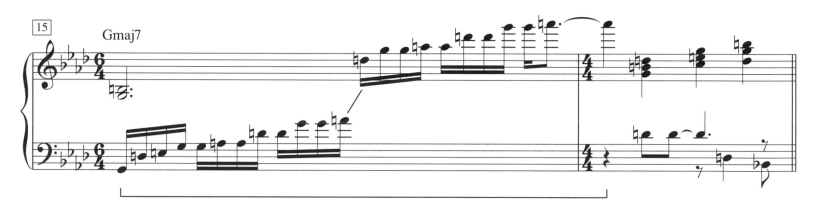

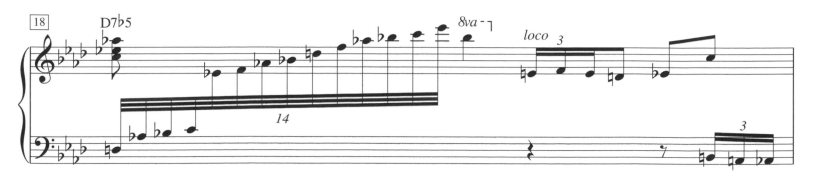

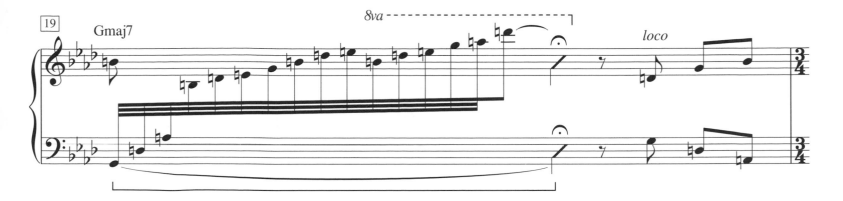

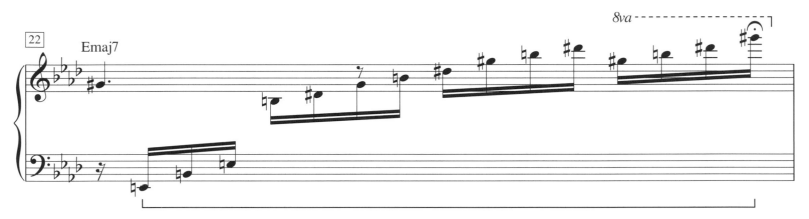

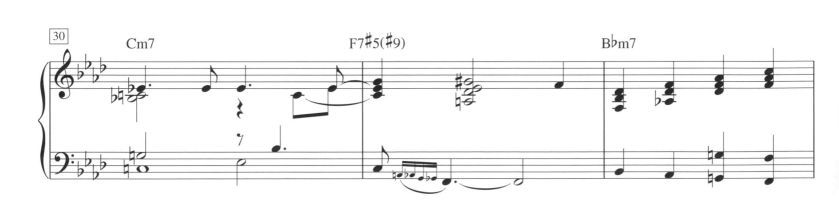

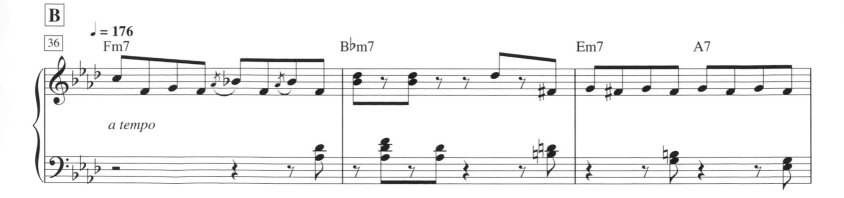

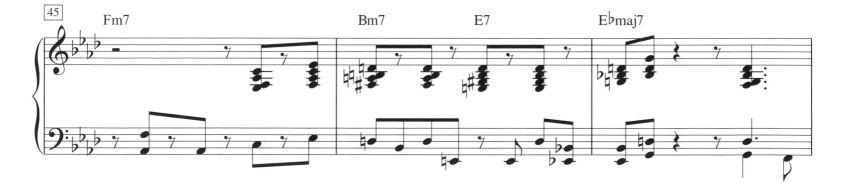

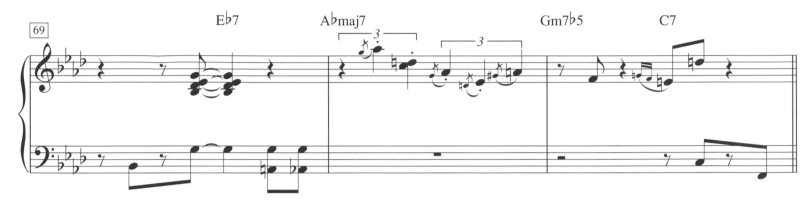

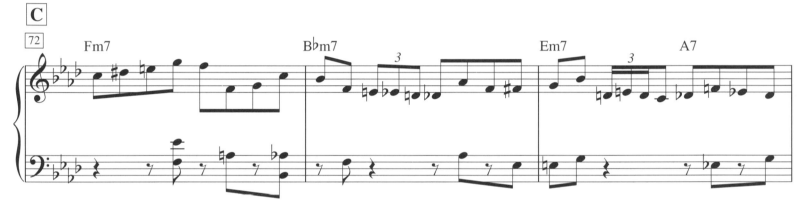

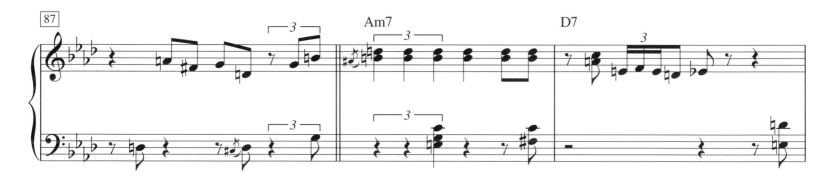

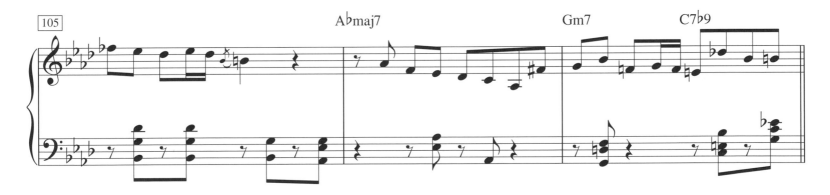

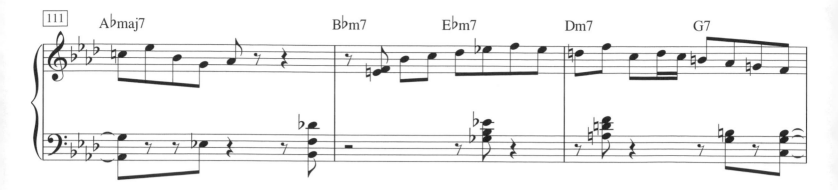

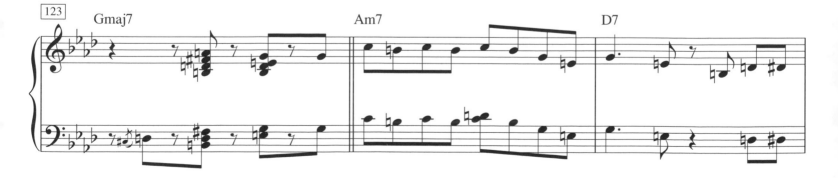

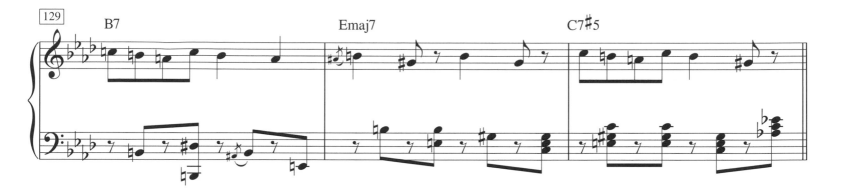

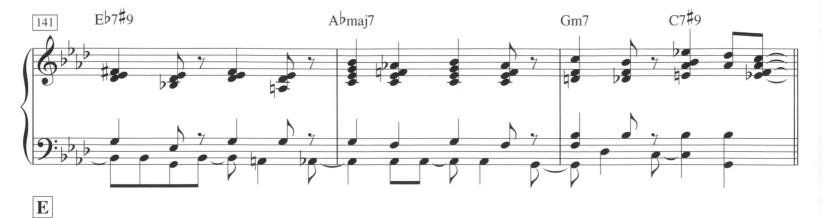

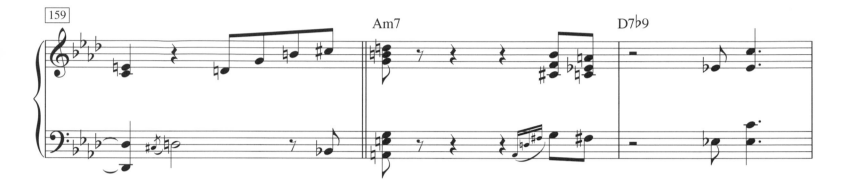

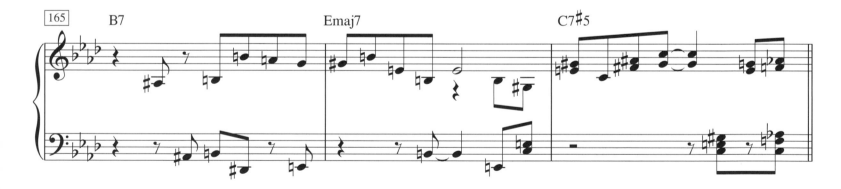

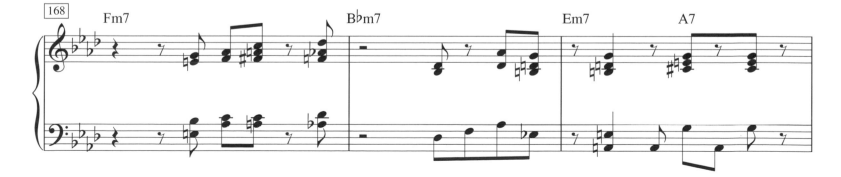

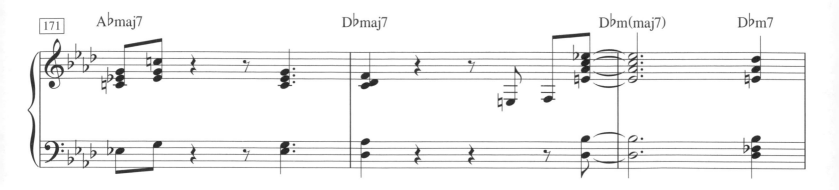

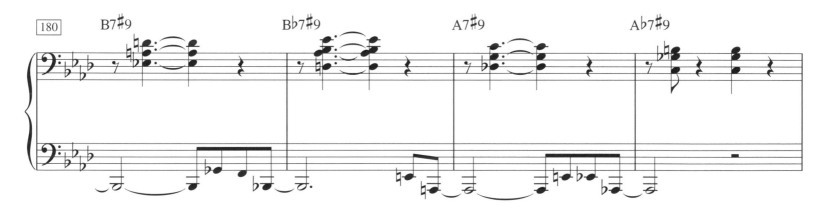

RALPH SHARON'S SOLO

An accompanist's accompanist, London-born Ralph Sharon has been providing backgrounds for major singers since he crossed the Big Pond in 1953. His choice of repertoire when performing as a soloist/leader is, not surprisingly, standards-centric. On his recording of "All the Things You Are," Sharon brings to the table a long and distinguished career dedicated to face-lifting the Great American Songbook.

The reading of the verse (Figure 2, letter A) is fairly straightforward. Raising the sheet music key of G major a semitone proves to call no undue attention to itself and allows a seamless entry into F minor where an eight-bar vamp sets a fast tempo. Sharon's head at letter B includes some intriguing subtlties: a) G♭, the flatted fifth of the prevailing C major 7 chord (bars 7–8) is ground first against an F and then, more pleasingly, against an E; b) bar 9's minor chord hides D, its ninth, in the bowels of the voicing, a dramatic sound; c) bars 21–22 use a minor seventh with a flatted fifth (Kern's original chord choice), one of the few cases of agreement with the composer on that critical point among the soloists in this book.

Letter C's well-mannered bebop is not without a few surprises. We meet again with the sonorous low placement of the ninth in bar 9, and the chords from bars 9–16, with one exception, are presented in rootless voicings. At bars 7–8 the lines before the recap are snake-hipped enough to avoid the jagged corners of a circle of fifths.

The final chorus at F traffics in a six-bar motif stressing the last upbeat of each bar throughout the main strain. Stated twice, each occurrence is rounded off by a two-bar drum fill. Sharon recalls the vamp he introduced after the verse at letter G. Whether the descending chromatic octaves of the ending are a send-up of the kind of music for silent movies that accompanied mustachioed villains who foreclose on the mortgage or constitute a worthy jazz idea, is best left for the reader to decide.

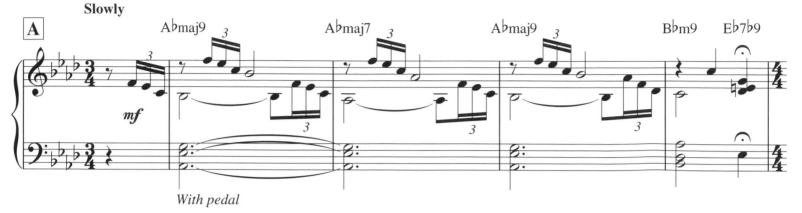

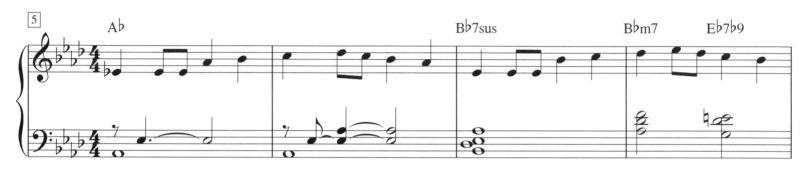

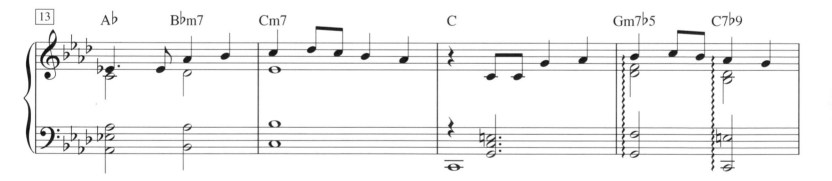

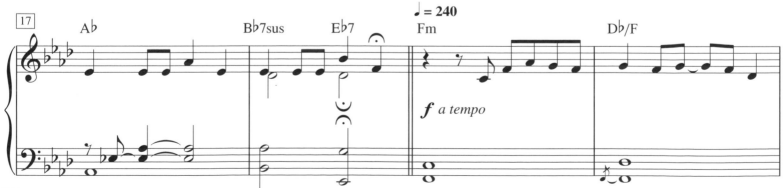

24

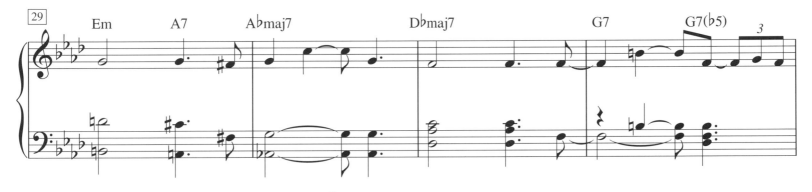

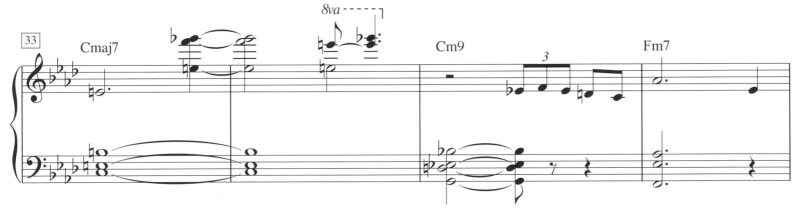

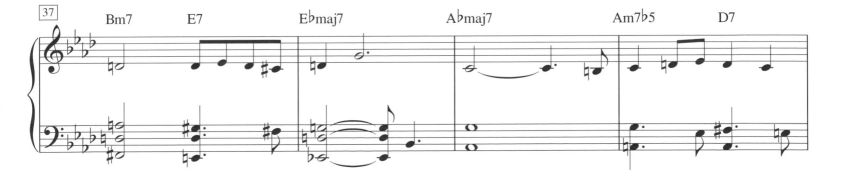

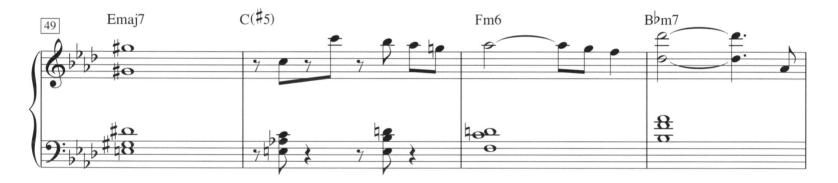

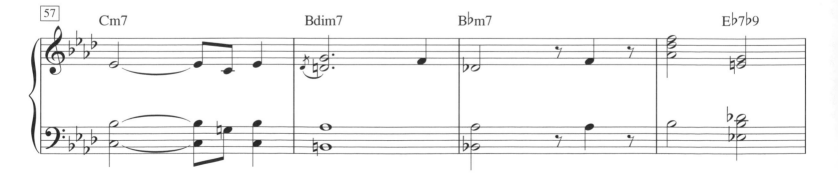

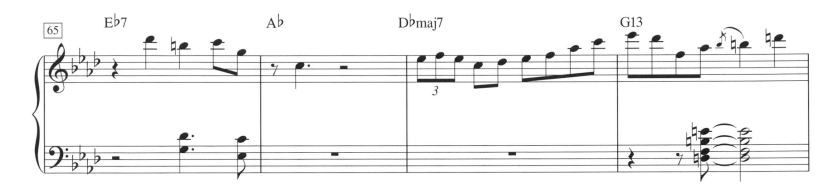

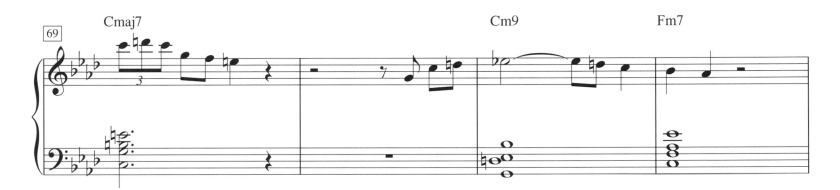

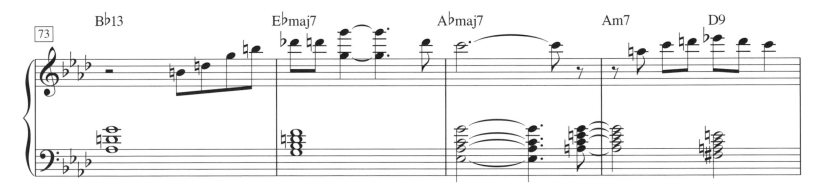

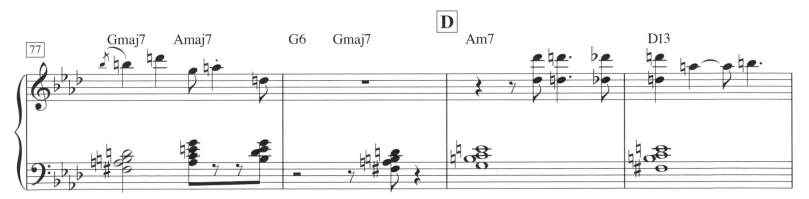

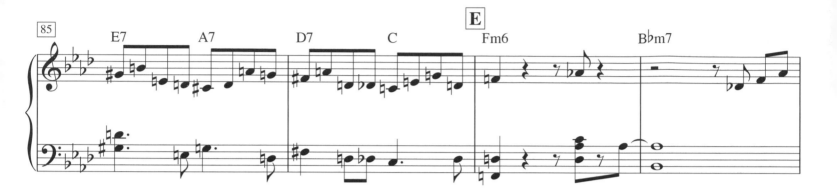

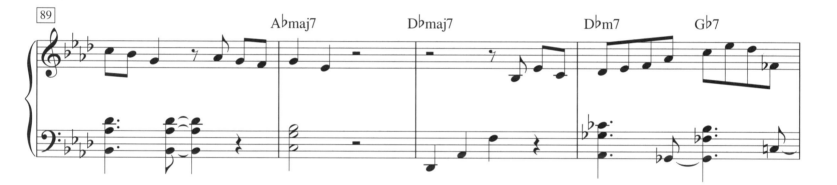

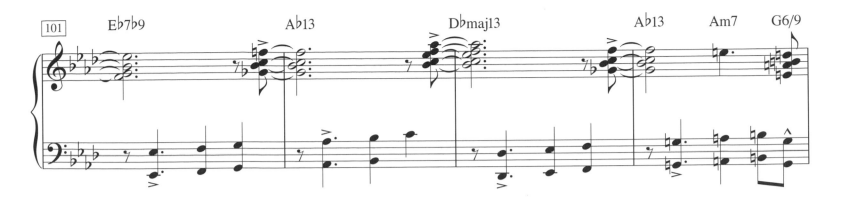

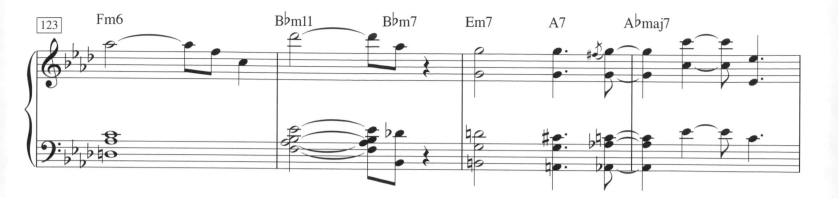

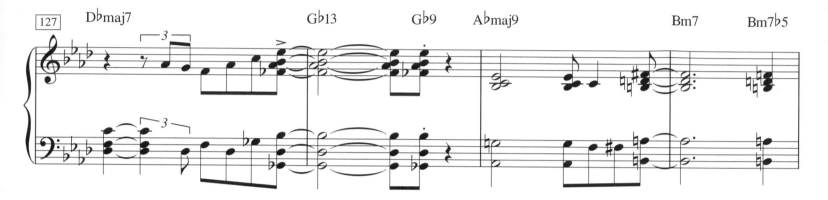

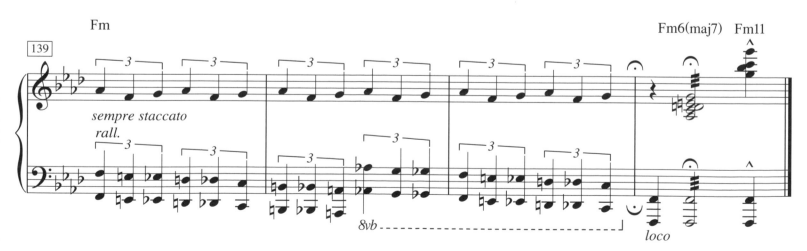

SOLOS (HEAD IN ONLY) BY DEREK SMITH AND MARIAN McPARTLAND

HEAD IN AS PLAYED BY DEREK SMITH

*S*mith is a capable pianist with clear ties to the Art Tatum/Oscar Peterson tradition. The British expatriate's cheerful exposition of "All the Things You Are" is consistent with his sunny treatment of standards.

A good deal of harmonic ground is covered in Figure 3 (bars 3–8). The rootless chords there require little movement within the same basic hand distribution to delineate the progressions. This section also boasts an alto voice that becomes a singable line of its own. There is similar hand-friendly activity and alto voice independence in bars 11–13. The fills (bars 7–8 and bar 16) are witty; Smith was, not for nothing, entrusted with "filling up the windows" in the charts during his five-year tenure with TV's *The Tonight Show* house band.

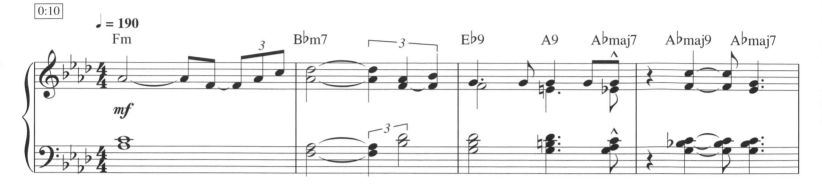

32

Oscar Peterson-like single notes anchor the left hand on upbeats in Figure 4, bars 3 and 4. The F♯m7♭5 (bar 5) is endorsed by Kern's sheet music.

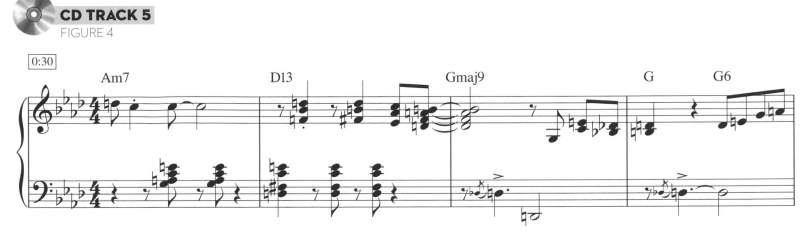

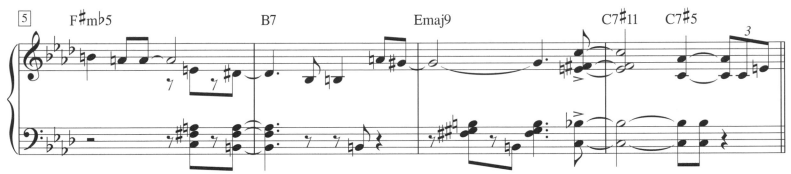

Smith opens Figure 5 with a sonorous minor 11th chord. There is a fresh twist on the melody in bar 10.

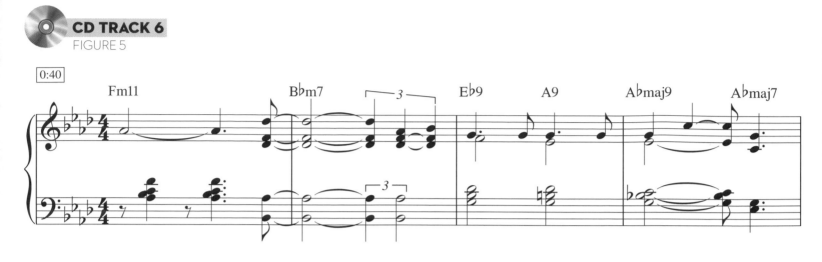

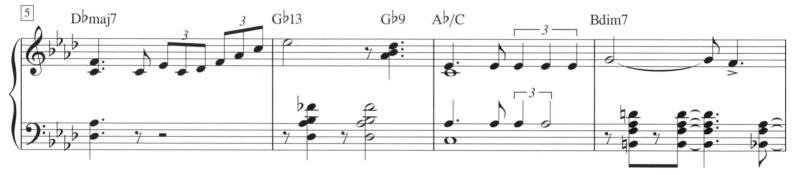

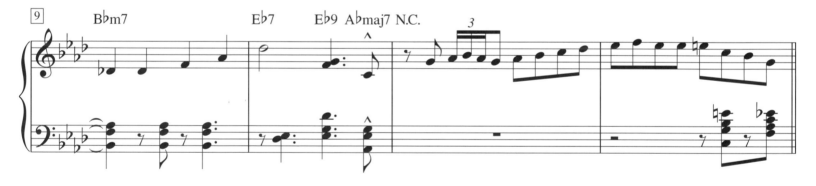

HEAD IN AS PLAYED BY MARIAN McPARTLAND

*S*ince settling stateside in 1946 as the British war bride of Dixieland cornetist Jimmy McPartland, Marian McPartland has always kept up with new developments in jazz. Figure 6 reflects her interest in younger players and confirms her roots in earlier styles. The opening chord stacked in fourths, and the dense inner voices of bar 10, bear witness to the influence of McCoy Tyner and other post-moderns, but treating the fourth beat of bars 2 and 9 with 13th chords is pure Art Tatum. McPartland takes liberties with the bar structure (another post-modern phenomenon), foreshortening the melody's longer note holds and skipping over a few repetitive non-essentials in the line. Semitonal bebop progressions were rampant on 52nd Street during the pianist's long stint at the Hickory House (1952–60), and she was all ears; witness bars 2–4 and 9–12.

0:22

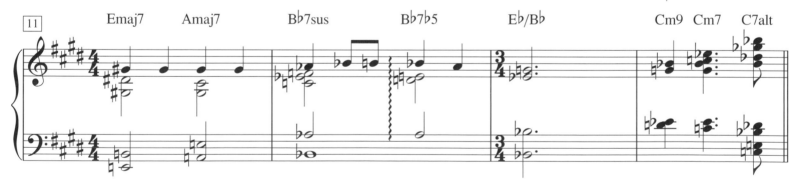

In interviews, McPartland has associated keys with colors. ("D is daffodil yellow, B major is maroon and B♭ is blue.") She is not on the record about the E♭ and C key centers in the bridge of this song (Figure 7), but they are most certainly approached with white heat. The fervent substitutions in the first bar contradict the II-V practice of legions of pianists and confirm the dominant chord of E♭ in bar 2 with a stunning tritone bass line. Taking advantage of the appoggiatura in the melody (bar 4), McPartland adds Ė, a major seventh, low in the voicing to intensify the moment. The crucial eighth bar is swathed in a Lydian dominant scale on B♭ (1 2 3 ♯4 5 6 ♭7 8).

CD TRACK 8
FIGURE 7

This solo's common application of the 6/4 chord (a chord in second inversion) can hardly escape notice. The voicing's very instability forecasts a strong follow-up, which McPartland always delivers. But never so effectively as the A♭ 6/4 she comes upon in bar 13 of Figure 8, which raises its bass note a semitone to the third of a C7 chord in bar 14. You can safely bet the farm on a modulation to F minor for the next chorus.

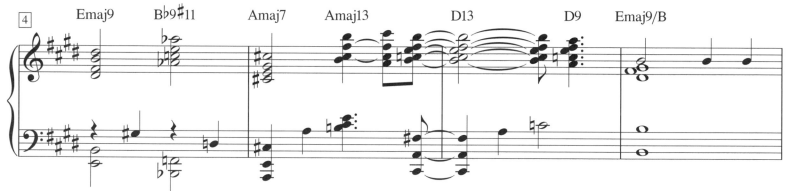

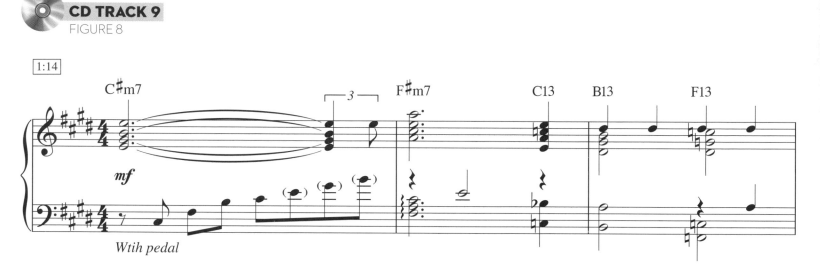

DOUBLE CHORUS IMPROVISATIONS AS PLAYED BY PHINEAS NEWBORN JR. AND DAVE BRUBECK

PHINEAS NEWBORN'S CHORUSES

$\mathcal{N}$ewborn's arrival on the jazz scene in the mid 1950s kicked many a Bud Powell wannabe to the curb. Powell himself was in decline when Newborn was recording solos with the masterful technique and cogent creativity shown in Figure 9. Fuller chord accompaniment, longer phrases, and effortless hand independence (the latter highlighted in the bridge, bars 17–24) are virtues which, then and now, set this artist apart from your father's bebop piano player. An intense, sober-minded musician who underwent the training of a concert pianist, the divided staccato octaves in bar 35 are as playful as Newborn gets. His feather-light touch, the antithesis of the more assertive Powell approach, in no way compromises a swinging groove.

CD TRACK 10
FIGURE 9

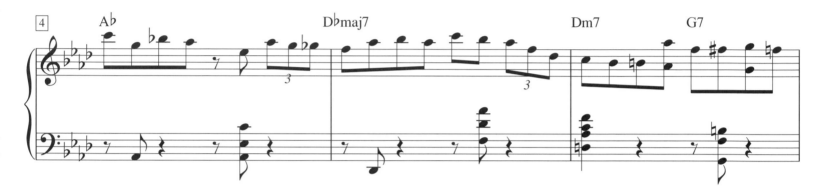

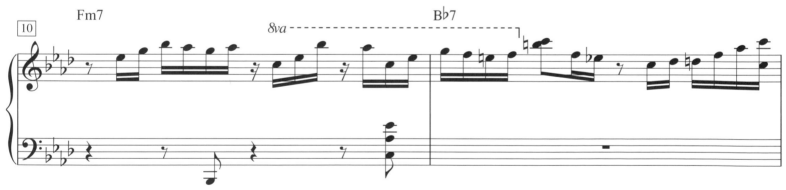

40

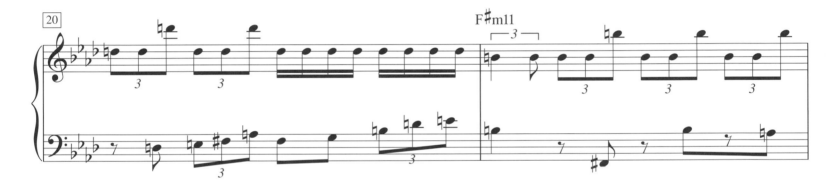

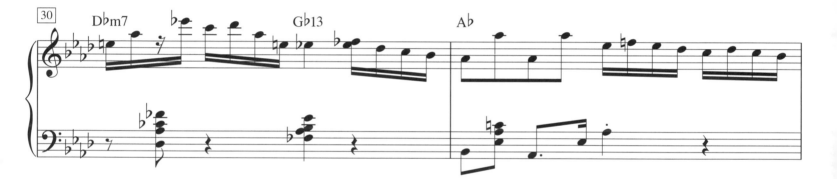

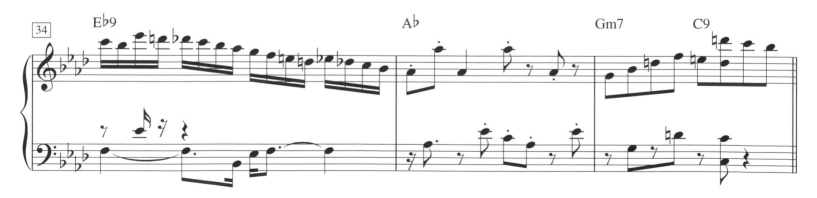

For a pianist with a reputation for weapons-grade chops, the first 16 bars of Figure 10 are technically unspectacular; eighth notes do most of the grunt work. Newborn, however, is far from merely phoning in an improvisation over Kern's circle of fifths. The opening lines form an integrated melodic statement eight bars long, not a loosely connected series of two-bar fragments of the sort usually dispensed by lower flying "Birds" on this segment of the tune. In bars 9–11, bristling octaves in both hands meet on the upbeats to set off primary chord tones.

Bars 19–21 sample Newborn's enviable double octave passagework. He sidesteps Kern's enharmonic turnaround at the end of the bridge (bar 24) with a II-V progression. Half of the remaining solo is executed with double-time ideas that tweak the higher extensions of the chords. Newborn stripped his playing of such agile moments in his last recordings to appease the critics who accused him of showy note-spinning. Many of the naysayers had once hailed him as the Second Coming.

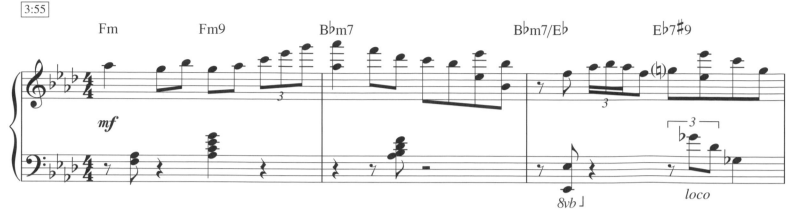

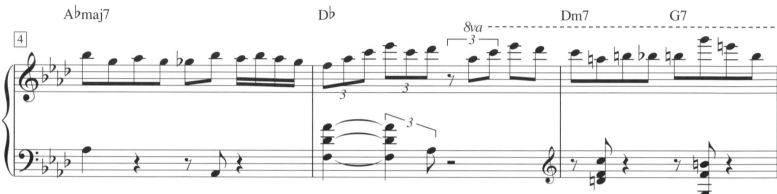

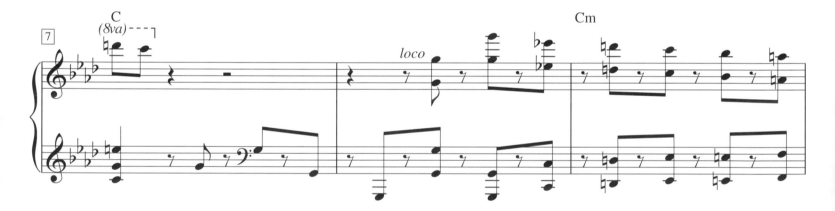

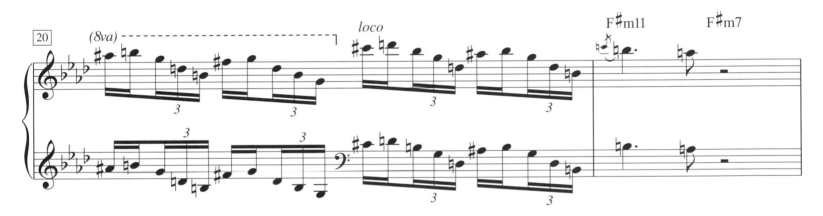

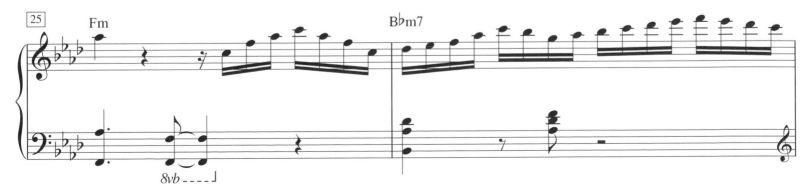

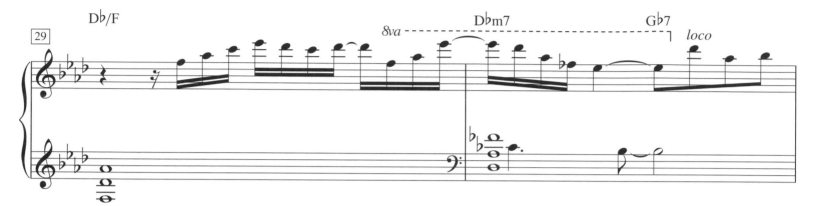

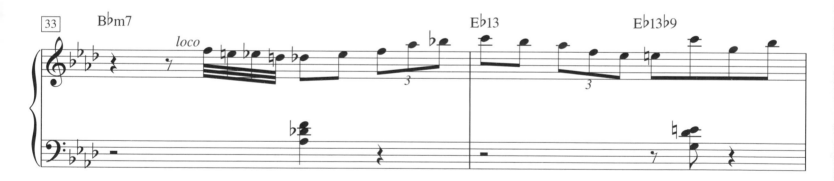

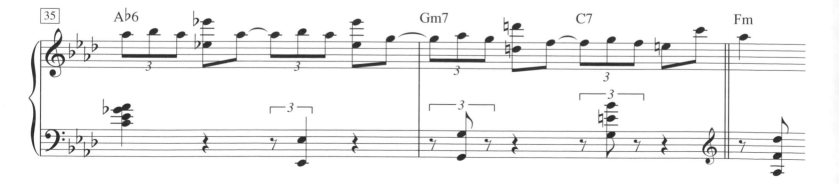

DAVE BRUBECK'S CHORUSES

$\mathscr{B}$rubeck, now a semi-retired octogenarian, is more than a half-century removed from this solo, recorded in 1953. The solo makes a strong case for citing Brubeck's pre-*Time Out* years as among the most creative of his long career. More recent developments in jazz have blunted the performance's sharper corners, but it still yields an impact on Kern's magnum opus in unconventional ways.

Two bars in Figure 11 feature significant harmonic clashes: Bar 3 presents an E♭7 with the third and a suspended fourth simultaneously; Bar 30 is in conflict as to whether C or C♭ prevails to qualify the chord as a D♭maj7 or D♭7. Six-part chords with interesting doublings (which avant-garde pianist Cecil Taylor has reluctantly admitted once drew him to Brubeck) loom in bars 14, 21, and 34. The turnaround at the end of the bridge defies convention, if only because it quotes Kern's original harmony almost verbatim. Bars 25–31 obsess over a quarter note triplet motif, but varied accompaniment leavens any danger of tedium.

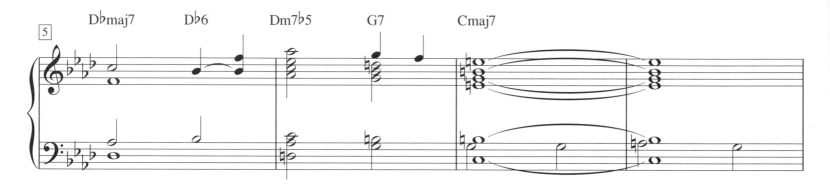

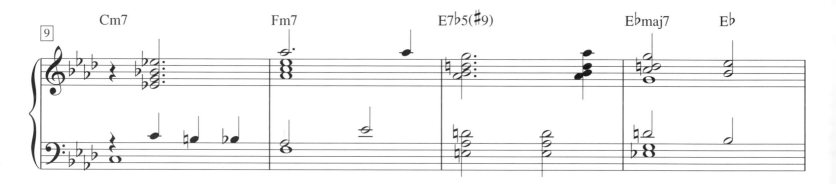

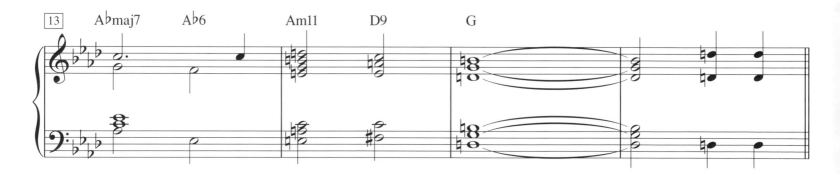

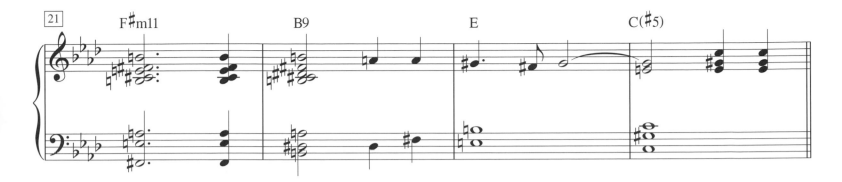

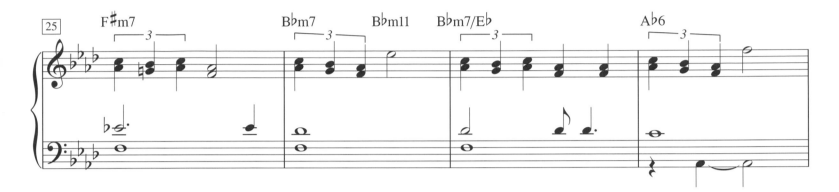

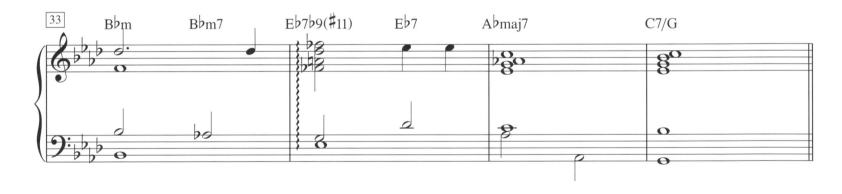

Brubeck invests more rhythmic capital in his second chorus than he did in the first. He has never been a soloist who hits the ground running. Some canny syncopations turn up the heat in Figure 12. The upbeat tie to a downbeat between bars 3 and 4, makes a strong pivot for an eight-bar shout figure at mid-point. A jaunty riff that requires hardly any melodic alterations covers the chord changes in bars 11–14.

The chorus's crowning achievement is the last 12 bars, where chord tones in the line are approached and left by a series of achingly beautiful whole and/or half-step appoggiaturas.

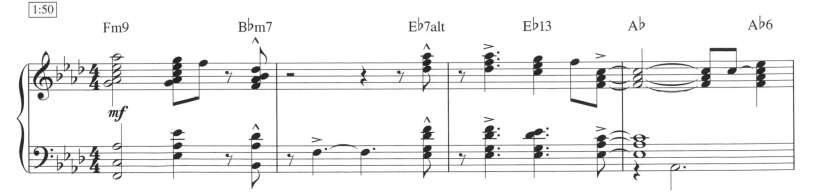

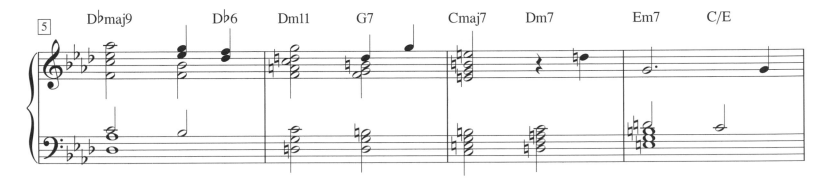

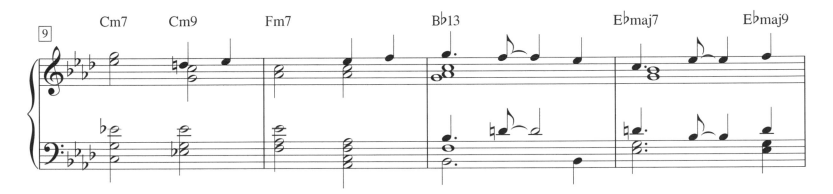

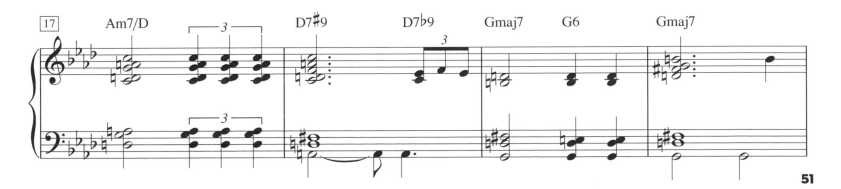

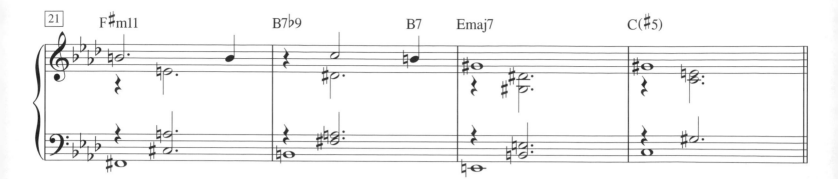

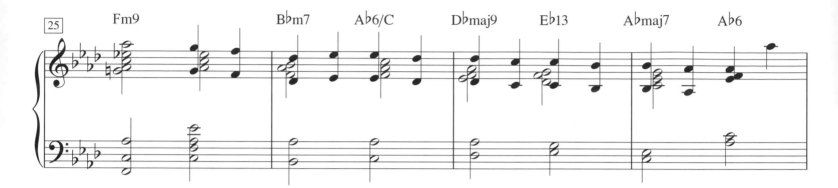

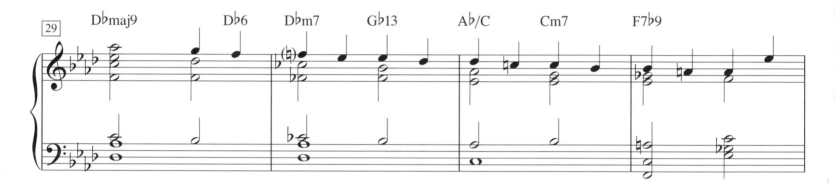

IMPROVISED BRIDGES AS PLAYED BY ANDRÉ PREVIN, OSCAR PETERSON, AND ADAM MAKOWICZ

ANDRÉ PREVIN'S BRIDGE

This is an inside solo masquerading as an outside one. The icy dissonances in the right hand are more closely related to the chord changes than they seem to be. Close inspection shows that their most contentious intervals (the upbeats of bars 2, 4, 5, and 6) are no further than the distance of a seventh from the root. And the important chord qualifying third is always present in the accompaniment. Previn is a master of such sheep-in-wolf's-clothing shenanigans. The solo from which this is excerpted appears on Previn's 1989 recording *After Hours*, which marked his return to jazz after nearly 30 years of working exclusively as a conductor of symphony orchestras.

CD TRACK 14
FIGURE 13

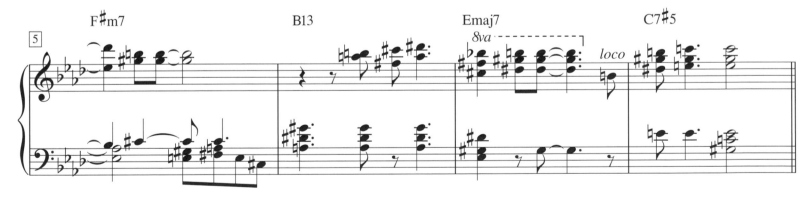

OSCAR PETERSON'S BRIDGE

*A*lthough best known for his lightning fast single-note technique, Peterson can also be an ingenious harmonist, as shown in Figure 14. The last of the quarter note triplets in bar 1 features one of his characteristic dominant sevenths with a flatted fifth. Its peculiar voicing (two tritones) permits the lower tritone to move to the third and seventh of the next chord by a mere semitonal drop. The upper tritone behaves similarly, to good advantage. Kern's somewhat predictable four-bar sequences are less sharply defined by Peterson's harmony. The pianist's refusal to be confined by G major in bar 3 is manifest by a defiant reference to A♭. The resistance to E major (bar 7) is even more pronounced; the third (G♯) is delayed for a beat and a half.

CD TRACK 15
FIGURE 14

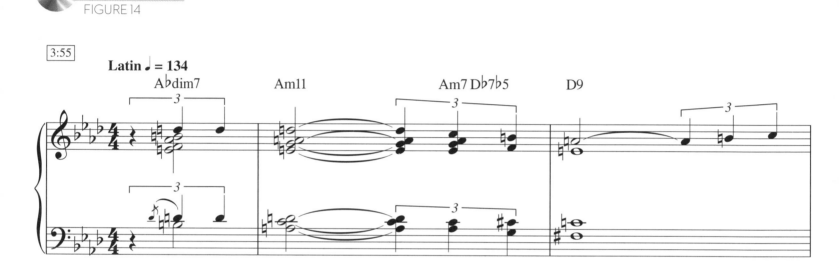

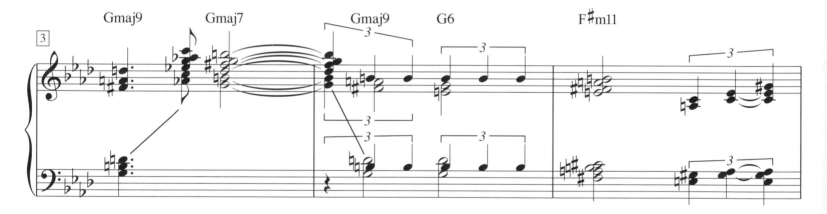

ADAM MAKOWICZ'S BRIDGE

*M*akowicz is one of jazz impresario John Hammond's later discoveries. Nothing in Figure 15 attests to the Polish-American pianist's former affiliations with Eastern European fusion. The style is decidedly mainstream, but of a more two-handed sort than is generally heard. From bars 1–6, restless lines are almost on equal terms with a rather fulsome accompaniment. Only the lines in bars 6–8 upstage their harmonic braces, either by recruiting some prickly extensions (bar 6) or, by contrast, against less active support (bars 7–8).

The end of the bridge proves what a minefield Kern's turnaround can be. Makowicz, in the heat of the moment, overshoots an obligatory C chord, or some reasonable facsimile, by a semitone (the C#9 in bar 8). The miscalculation costs him almost eight bars of backpedaling in F# minor to claim the proper key of F minor.

CD TRACK 16
FIGURE 15

INTROS AS PLAYED BY JOE ALBANY, AHMAD JAMAL, HAL SCHAEFFER, AND TOMMY FLANAGAN

JOE ALBANY'S INTRO

This intro first appeared on Charlie Parker's 1947 recording of "All the Things You Are," better known as "Bird of Paradise." Quoting it in front before stating Kern's theme has become a tradition in jazz ever since. Here, with a few modifications of Duke Jordan's original piano part, is the venerable preamble as recycled by bebop legend Joe Albany.

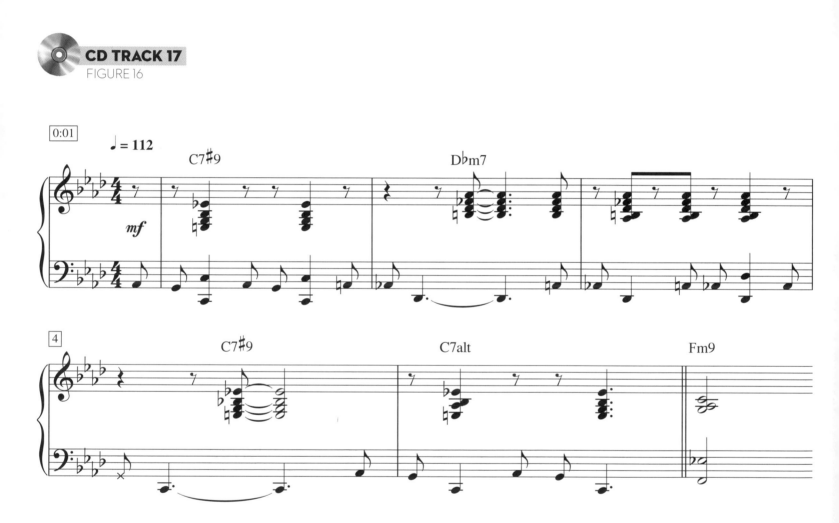

CD TRACK 17
FIGURE 16

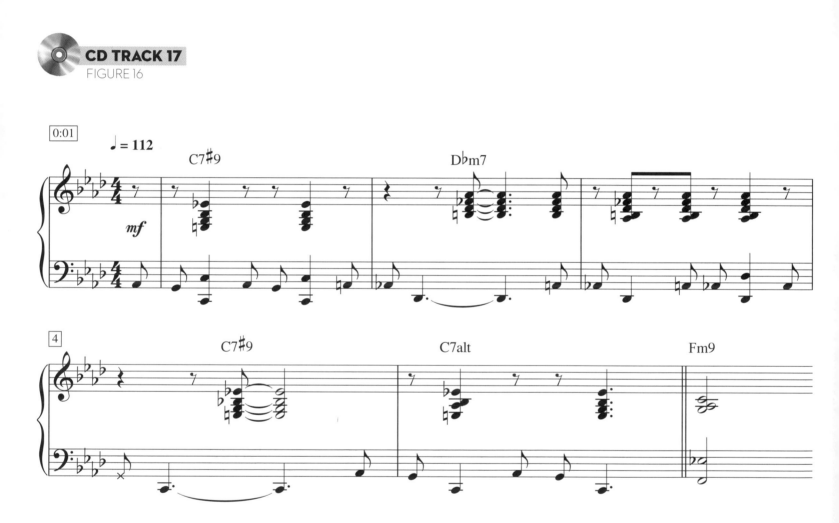

AHMAD JAMAL'S INTRO

*J*amal walks a fine line between citing Parker's intro and exercising his own subtle originality. His right hand stresses the classic semitonal progression on the proper upbeats, but the expected sharp ninth chords have been recast as suspended dominant sevenths. Jamal feels no obligation to add the roots of the chords to the bass line. Instead, he opts for second inversion voicings (fifths in the bass) that give a floating quality to the harmony. The last half of bar 8 outlines a Gm7 to C13 progression in free two-part counterpoint.

CD TRACK 18
FIGURE 17

HAL SCHAEFFER'S INTRO

*T*here are no allusions to the "Bird of Paradise" in the plain-spoken bebop of Figure 18. Veteran pianist/composer Hal Schaeffer (*Downbeat* poll winner, New Star category, 1945) clings to the tonic and dominant of A♭ major in the first four bars. (The C7♯9 in bar 3 is a red herring. It does not act as a secondary dominant to F minor, and deftly proceeds to reclaim the tonic.) Schaeffer throws the thirds of the chords in high relief on the third beats of bars 5 and 6. Their location within rhythmically identical lines is clearly stressed. An emphatic octave C (bar 8) brings all harmonic activity to a screeching halt, which sets the stage for Kern's relentless circle of fifths ahead.

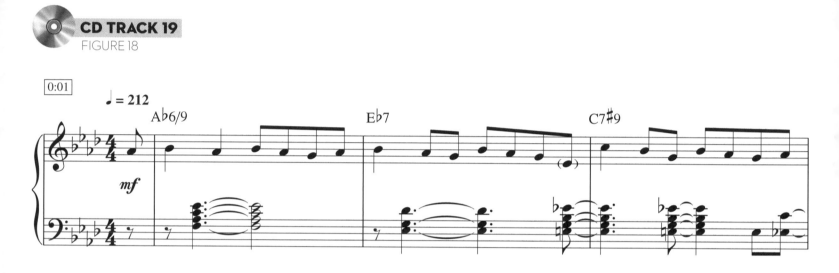

CD TRACK 19
FIGURE 18

TOMMY FLANAGAN'S INTRO

*F*lanagan's intro is in tribute to Parker's only insofar as the chords are basically the same. True to form, Flanagan, the most elegant stylist of the Detroit school, appropriates Parker's chords without their fidgety rhythmic trappings. Presentations of the original semitonal progression now appear on the downbeat in a relaxed accompaniment vibe while the right hand gets off some tangy licks. The tendency to play over all the scenes of the two-bar phrase construction is nicely averted; Flanagan is too shrewd an improviser not to give his lines a breather on the initial beats of bars 3 and 7.

CD TRACK 20
FIGURE 19

LAST 12 AND ENDING PLAYED BY CEDAR WALTON AND SHELLY BERG

CEDAR WALTON'S LAST 12 AND ENDING

*A*lthough Figure 20 is not a literal recap, Walton takes pains to keep Kern's essentials in his crosshairs. The melody is amended by tied anticipations and selective passing tones that unobtrusively frost the line with the kind of hard bop irony peculiar to this pianist. Walton's loyalty to the original harmony is almost obsessive. He includes, for example, the composer's diminished chord in bars 7–8, the only relief Kern offers from a continual circle of fifths.

Bar 11 begins a demonstration of how Charlie Parker's milestone intro for "Bird of Paradise" can also provide a good exit strategy for this tune. The solo concludes with a diminished scale wistfully spiraling upward into the piano's altissimo register.

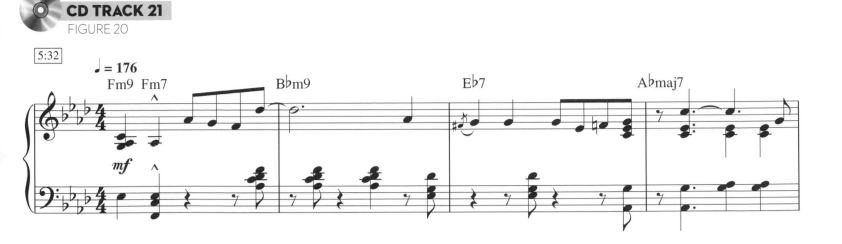

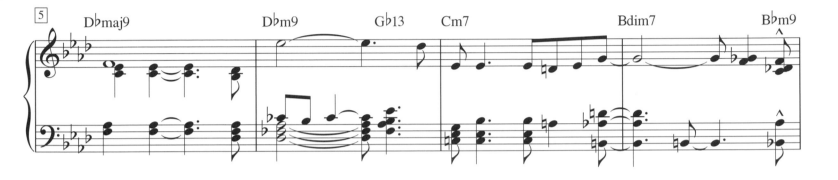

With pedal

SHELLY BERG'S LAST 12 AND ENDING

$\mathscr{B}$erg takes the final corridor of Kern's tour de force at medium up-tempo. A sideman with Texas tenor giant Arnett Cobb before joining the teaching staff of the University of Southern California's jazz studies department in the early 1990s, Berg manages to wade waist-deep in jazz tradition without sacrificing one whit of his finely honed classical technique. The pianist is too much his own man to indulge in slavish imitation, but the boppish lick—beginning on the upbeat of 2 in bar 5 of Figure 21 and ending on the downbeat of bar 7—bears the unmistakable stamp of his idol Oscar Peterson. A tag (bars 11–14) seems headed for another pass through the same circle of fifths, until the sharp nine chord on the subdominant at bar 15 sounds a heads-up for the celebrated "Bird of Paradise" intro/coda. Berg keeps the bloom on the rose of the potentially over-familiar eight-bar quote by moving the top voice of each paired four-bar division in ascending whole steps.

63

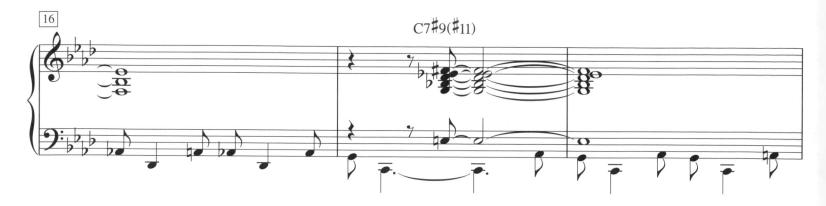

DISCOGRAPHY

(listed by artist)

ALBANY, JOE   *The Right Combination*, Ojc B000000Z61

BERG, SHELLY   *Blackbird*, Concord Records B00070EBC6

BRUBECK, DAVE   *Dave Brubeck Stardust*, Fantasy B000000XFK

FLANAGAN, TOMMY   *You're Me*, Phontastic B0005YA1F

HAWES, HAMPTON   *Hampton Hawes Trio*, Vol.1, Ojc B000000YHG

JAMAL, AHMAD   *Chicago Revisited Live at Joe Segal's Showcase*, Telarc B000003D3Q

MAKOWICZ, ADAM   *The Music of Jerome Kern*, Avid Records UK B000054BFQ

McPARTLAND, MARIAN   *Live at Shanghai Jazz*, Concord Records B000069COW

NEWBORN, PHINEAS JR.   *Here Is Phineas*, Collectables B0002S94S4

PETERSON, OSCAR   *Two Originals: Walking The Line/Another Day*, Polygram Records B000004764

PREVIN, ANDRÉ   *After Hours*, Telarc B000003D31

SCHAEFFER, HAL   *Solo*, Duo, Trio, Discovery/Wea B00000BOZW

SHARON, RALPH   *The Magic of Jerome Kern*, Avid Records UK B000054BFQ

SMITH, DEREK   *The Derek Smith Trio Plays Jerome Kern*, Progressive Records B000001DEG

WALTON, CEDAR   *Cedar Walton-Ron Carter-Jack DeJohnette*, Baystate 8085

CD TRACK LISTING

1   original sheet music

2   Hampton Hawes (solo)

3   Ralph Sharon (solo)

4   Derek Smith (head in)

5   Derek Smith

6   Derek Smith

7   Marian McPartland (head in)

8   Marian McPartland

9   Phineas Newborn Jr. (chorus)

10   Phineas Newborn Jr.

11   Phineas Newborn Jr.

12   Dave Brubeck (chorus)

13   Dave Brubeck

14   André Previn (bridge)

15   Oscar Peterson (bridge)

16   Adam Makowicz (bridge)

17   Joe Albany (intro)

18   Ahmad Jamal (intro)

19   Hal Schaeffer (intro)

20   Tommy Flanagan (intro)

21   Cedar Walton (last 12/ending)

22   Shelly Berg (last 12/ending)